Ebola

ANN O. SQUIRE

Children's Press®
An Imprint of Scholastic Inc.

Content Consultant

Karen E. Peters, DrPH
Clinical Assistant Professor
Division of Community Health Sciences
University of Illinois–Chicago, School of Public Health
Chicago, Illinois

Library of Congress Cataloging-in-Publication Data
Squire, Ann O., author.
 Ebola / by Ann O. Squire.
     pages cm. — (A true book)
 Includes bibliographical references and index.
 ISBN 978-0-531-21469-5 (library binding : alk. paper) — ISBN 978-0-531-21519-7 (pbk. : alk. paper)
 1. Ebola virus disease—Juvenile literature. 2. Hemorrhagic diseases—Juvenile literature.
 3. Epidemics—Juvenile literature. I. Title. II. Series: True book.
 RC140.5.S68 2016
 616.9'1—dc23   2015003991

© 2016 Scholastic Inc.
All rights reserved. Published in 2016 by Children's Press, an imprint of Scholastic Inc.
Printed in China 62
SCHOLASTIC, CHILDREN'S PRESS, A TRUE BOOK™, and associated logos are trademarks and/or registered trademarks of Scholastic Inc.
1 2 3 4 5 6 7 8 9 10 R 25 24 23 22 21 20 19 18 17 16

Front cover: A health-care worker in a protective suit in Monrovia, Liberia

Back cover: Ebola information in a school in Africa

Find the Truth!

Everything you are about to read is true *except* for one of the sentences on this page.

Which one is **TRUE**?

T or F The Ebola virus can be spread only among humans.

T or F The 2014 Ebola outbreak in West Africa was the worst one in history.

Find the answers in this book.

3

Contents

THE BIG TRUTH!

Ebola in the United States

**Scientists use microscopes to
magnify tiny viruses like Ebola.**

Ebola can spread if people exposed to the disease travel.

4 Treating Ebola

5 What the Future Holds

Ebola spreads through direct contact with infected blood or other body fluids.

5

Emile's father poses near the bat tree where the 2014 Ebola outbreak is believed to have started.

CHAPTER 1

A Deadly Beginning

In a forest near the tiny village of Meliandou, in the West African country of Guinea, there is a hollow tree that is home to a colony of bats. Children often play in and around the tree. Sometimes they catch the bats and release them into the sky. One day late in 2013, a two-year-old boy named Emile joined his friends at the bat tree for an afternoon of fun.

Bats may be the source of the 2014 Ebola outbreak in West Africa.

Sickness Spreads

A few days later, Emile began to feel sick. His mother and grandmother cared for him, but soon his fever and vomiting got worse. In late December, Emile died of his illness. The family mourned their son, but their problems were not over. Soon after the toddler's death, his mother started having symptoms. His grandmother and three-year-old sister got sick as well.

Emile's father looks at photos of family members he lost to Ebola.

Emile's home village of Meliandou was greatly affected by the Ebola outbreak.

Within a month, everyone in Emile's family was dead except for his father. At the time, no one in the village knew what had killed them. They arranged funerals and washed the bodies to prepare them for burial. Friends and relatives from other villages traveled to Meliandou to pay their respects. Without realizing it, some of those people caught the same illness that Emile and his family had. They unknowingly carried it back to their own villages.

Women gather in Liberia to pray that the Ebola outbreak ends.

A Major Problem

When they began to feel ill, some people went
to hospitals for treatment. The illness passed to
doctors and health-care workers. The sickness was
spreading fast. Just one and a half years later, more
than 25,000 cases of the disease—now identified
as Ebola **virus**—had occurred in the West African
countries of Guinea, Liberia, and Sierra Leone. By the
middle of 2015, more than 10,000 people had died.

How Is Ebola Transmitted?

Some viruses can be transmitted through the air. If someone who has a cold sneezes in your direction, you may come down with a cold as well. Ebola spreads only through direct contact with body fluids such as blood or saliva. If body fluid from an infected person gets in your eyes or mouth or an open wound, you may become infected. Ebola can also be spread through mistakes in a hospital or laboratory. Hospitals and labs that deal with Ebola have strict rules and regulations to prevent the accidental spread of the virus.

Health-care workers wear protective suits and masks while dealing with Ebola patients.

At first, doctors did not realize that some of their patients had Ebola.

Clinics in rural African villages lack many of the resources of hospitals in more developed areas.

CHAPTER 2

The Spread of Ebola

When doctors in West Africa first began to see patients with the strange illness, they did not **diagnose** them with Ebola. In the past, there had been several Ebola outbreaks in other parts of Africa, but the disease had never reached West Africa. So when doctors in Guinea began to see sick patients, they did not at first think of Ebola. Fever and other early symptoms of Ebola are also seen in patients with diseases such as malaria and typhoid fever. As a result, doctors did not take the proper steps to keep Ebola from spreading.

Secretly Sick

Ebola's incubation period can be as long as 21 days. An incubation period is the time it takes for a person who contracts a virus to show symptoms. It is possible that someone infected with Ebola might not feel sick for several weeks. Even after symptoms first appear, it can take a few days before the virus is detected in a person's blood.

An Ebola survivor brings his daughter to be tested for the disease.

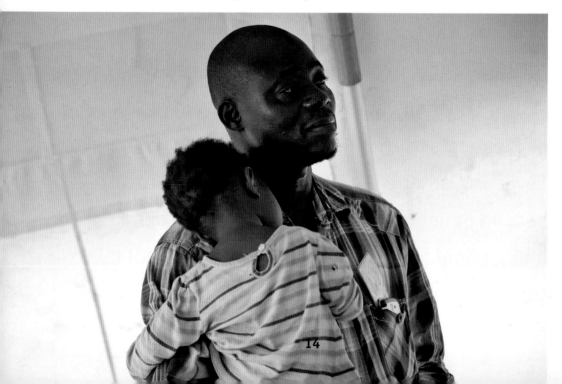

The Ebola virus can spread farther when infected people take airplanes or travel long distances in some other way before they knew they are sick.

Someone can be infected with Ebola and then travel a great distance before beginning to feel sick. Doctors didn't recognize the first cases of the disease as Ebola. This gave the virus time to spread throughout West Africa and beyond. The United States and several European countries have treated patients who traveled there after catching Ebola in Africa.

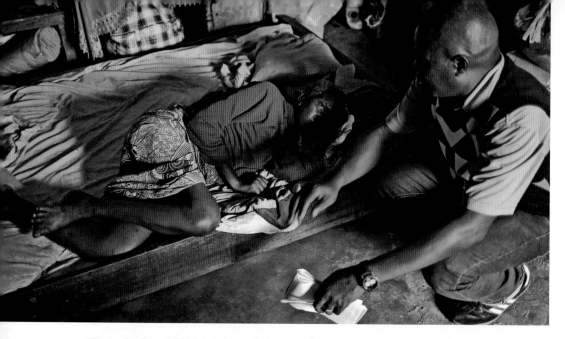

Ebola is incredibly contagious, so it is dangerous to care for a patient with Ebola without proper protective clothing and equipment.

Another reason for Ebola's spread was that West Africa's small regional clinics lacked basic protective clothing and supplies such as rubber gloves. This resulted in many health-care workers contracting the virus while caring for patients. It was not until March 2014 that the World Health Organization reported on the Ebola outbreak. This was more than two months after the deaths of Emile and his family.

Diagnosing Ebola

The symptoms of Ebola include fever, vomiting, headache, muscle and stomach pain, and, sometimes, unexplained bleeding. If a patient comes to a clinic with these symptoms, the doctor can do a blood test to look for signs of infection. Unfortunately, the virus can be passed along even before it is detectable in the bloodstream.

Doctors must be very careful when handling blood samples of patients who might have Ebola.

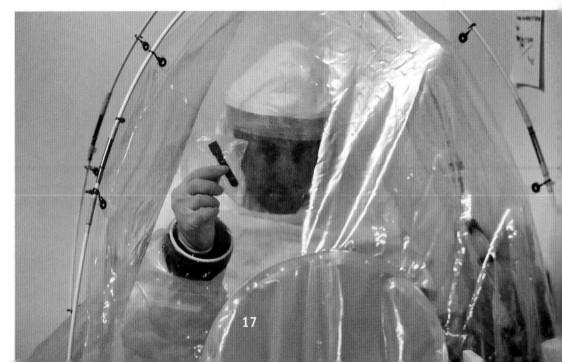

Keeping an Eye on Ebola

It is very important to keep a close watch on any suspected Ebola patient until doctors know for sure whether the person is infected. Some U.S. states **quarantined** health-care workers returning from countries where they might have cared for Ebola patients. Other states simply monitored the health status of workers until the 21-day incubation period had passed.

A patient sits in a quarantine area in a Maryland hospital.

A contact tracer speaks with the relatives of an Ebola patient in Africa.

Tracing the Contacts

To contain an Ebola outbreak, it's not enough to diagnose patients or keep them away from others. The virus's long incubation period means that an infected person could have passed on the disease to many people before coming to a clinic. Health-care workers ask patients for a list of people with whom they spent time during this period. They then contact everyone on the list and monitor them for Ebola symptoms for 21 days. This is called contact tracing. If even one person is missed, the **epidemic** may keep spreading.

Ebola got its name from the Ebola River, which was near the center of one of the first outbreaks of the disease.

CHAPTER 3

Searching for a Source

Ebola is a deadly disease caused by a type of virus. Five different versions of the Ebola virus have been identified. Four of these cause illness in humans as well as other **primates**, such as chimpanzees, monkeys, and gorillas. The first recorded outbreak of Ebola occurred in South Sudan (then part of Sudan) in June 1976. It then spread to Zaire (now the Democratic Republic of the Congo) in September 1976.

Bats have been linked to multiple zoonoses, including rabies and Ebola.

Zoonosis

Ebola is a zoonosis. This means it is a disease that can be transmitted from animals to people. Other examples of zoonoses are rabies (transmitted by infected animals such as bats), Lyme disease (ticks), and avian influenza (birds such as chickens and ducks). With some of these diseases, the animal **host** also becomes ill.

With other zoonotic diseases, including Ebola, an animal carries the virus but is not sickened by it. This makes it difficult to tell which animals are hosting the disease. An animal that can carry a disease and pass it on to humans is known as a reservoir host. Even after the virus has infected humans, it remains in the reservoir host. It hides in the bodies of the host animals, which remain unaffected by it.

Rats and other rodents can be reservoir hosts: they may carry diseases that can be transferred to humans.

Finding the Reservoir Host

Ever since the first Ebola outbreak in 1976, scientists have been trying to find the reservoir host species for this deadly virus. Gorillas, chimps, and other primates often die of the virus after contracting it. This told scientists that the reservoir host must be an animal that comes into contact with forest primates as well as people.

Ebola transmission from animals to humans can occur when people eat the meat of an infected animal. It can even occur if they eat something that has come into contact with body fluids of an infected animal. The virus can also be transmitted through animal bites. Most Ebola outbreaks have started in rural areas near forests, giving scientists a clue that a forest animal is probably the reservoir host. But which one?

Major Ebola Outbreaks in Africa

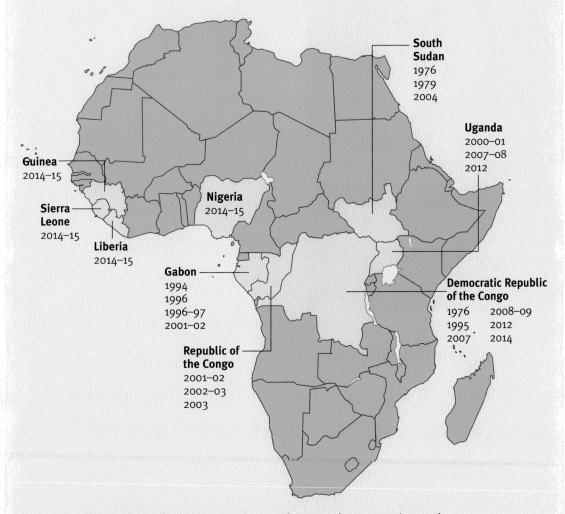

South Sudan
1976
1979
2004

Uganda
2000–01
2007–08
2012

Guinea
2014–15

Nigeria
2014–15

Sierra Leone
2014–15

Liberia
2014–15

Gabon
1994
1996
1996–97
2001–02

Democratic Republic of the Congo

1976	2008–09
1995	2012
2007	2014

Republic of the Congo
2001–02
2002–03
2003

This map includes countries and years that experienced outbreaks with 10 or more confirmed cases.

Scientists tested monkeys and other animals to locate the Ebola reservoir host.

A Fruitless Search

After a 1995 Ebola outbreak in the Democratic Republic of the Congo, scientists did an ambitious study aimed at finding Ebola's reservoir host. Working in a forest area near where the outbreak occurred, they trapped nearly 3,000 mammals, birds, reptiles, and amphibians. After testing all the animals for the Ebola virus, they were disappointed to find that none were infected. The search for the reservoir host continued.

Bats?

Recently, scientists have begun to suspect that bats may be spreading the Ebola virus. Studies conducted elsewhere in Africa have shown that bats can carry Ebola. The children of Meliandou played near the bats in the hollow tree, and they sometimes caught the animals to cook and eat. If bats do turn out to be the reservoir host, scientists will be able to take a giant step toward controlling the spread of Ebola.

A researcher examines a bat that has been captured for Ebola studies.

Ebola in the United States

In September 2014, Thomas Eric Duncan prepared to board a plane in Liberia. He was going to Dallas, Texas, to visit family. At the airport, Duncan and other departing passengers went through a health screening. Duncan's temperature was normal. He answered "no" when asked if he'd had contact with any Ebola patients. Although he may not have known it, Duncan had been exposed to Ebola a few days earlier when he helped take a sick neighbor to the hospital.

Soon after his arrival in Dallas, Duncan began to feel ill and visited a hospital. Workers there did not recognize his symptoms as Ebola. He was treated and sent home. Soon his condition worsened. A few days later, he returned to the hospital by ambulance. This time, he was diagnosed with Ebola and isolated from other patients. He died just weeks later on October 8, 2014.

Duncan had contact with many family members and friends in the United States. He also had contact with hospital workers. Two nurses later tested positive for Ebola. Health officials tracked down the people he had spent time with. Some of them were quarantined for several weeks.

Fortunately, both nurses recovered, and no one else developed Ebola. But U.S. health officials learned how easy it is to miss Ebola symptoms and how many people can be affected if that happens.

When viewed under a microscope, the Ebola virus is revealed to have a long, thin shape.

CHAPTER 4

Treating Ebola

Ebola kills a large number of the people who become infected with it. The death rate in the 2014 West Africa outbreak has been estimated to be between 50 and 90 percent. To make matters worse, no medicines or treatments have been approved to combat the virus. However, several companies are working to develop drugs and **vaccines** that would cure or prevent Ebola.

 Ebola is one of the most deadly viruses in history.

A Disappearing Virus

One reason it has been so difficult to learn about the Ebola virus or to come up with effective treatments is that the virus seems to disappear in between human outbreaks. After the first outbreaks in the 1970s, no more Ebola cases were recorded in Africa for 15 years. This was good news for the people of Africa. However, it was frustrating for scientists hoping to learn more about the virus.

Life returns to normal during long periods between outbreaks.

Workers prepare medication for delivery to Ebola patients.

Stopping Ebola's Spread

Until drugs to cure and prevent Ebola are available, the best approach is to stop the virus from spreading from animals to people or from infected people to other people. This is difficult. One reason is that scientists aren't certain which animal carries the virus. Another is that the virus's long incubation period allows infected people to have contact with many others before showing symptoms. Also, the habits of some people in Africa put them at greater risk of contracting the disease.

A man in Gabon cooks a stew with lizard meat caught in the wild.

Hunting for Food

Handling or eating meat from infected animals is one way that the Ebola virus is spread. In rural parts of Africa, many people hunt and eat wild animals, including bats, deer, primates, and rats. This is particularly true when other food is scarce. Because Ebola affects monkeys and apes the same way it affects humans, eating those animals could be dangerous.

Caring for the Sick and Dead

The ways people care for the sick and bury their dead can also affect their chances of contracting Ebola. Taking care of a sick person traditionally involves a lot of bodily contact, including kissing and embracing. In some cultures, if the patient dies, it is customary to wash the person's body and to touch and kiss it before burial. Such customs allow the Ebola virus to spread in West Africa.

Liberian people attend a funeral in the capital city of Monrovia.

Changing Customs

Stopping the spread of Ebola begins with convincing people to change behaviors that put them at risk. Governments tell people in Africa to avoid eating bats and other animals. But food is scarce in many rural areas, and meat from wild animals is a good source of nutrition. With this in mind, some organizations encourage people to make sure they cook the meat very thoroughly. This helps kill potential diseases in the food.

Meat from animals that were hunted in the wild is sometimes sold at outdoor markets.

Workers transfer a body to a special cemetery set aside for Ebola victims.

It is equally difficult to change traditions regarding the sick and dying. Throughout West Africa, specialized burial teams have been sent out to deal with Ebola-infected bodies. Wearing protective clothing, workers disinfect the bodies with bleach before burying or **cremating** them. It is an unpleasant job, but the hardest part is convincing relatives of the dead person that it is important to keep their distance.

A health worker explains the need to be careful to family members of an Ebola victim.

Superstitions

Many residents of isolated African villages are superstitious about Ebola. Some believe the disease is a result of witchcraft or sorcery. Others believe that health-care workers who came to help were actually the ones who brought Ebola to their communities.

Stopping a Killer

Developing new treatments for disease usually takes many years. But during the Ebola crisis, governments and drug companies raced to come up with better ways to diagnose and treat Ebola. One promising drug called ZMapp works to pinpoint the virus and neutralize it. Two American aid workers who contracted Ebola were the first humans to receive the experimental drug. Both of them recovered. ZMapp is still in short supply, but it could eventually be one key to stopping Ebola in its tracks.

A doctor examines a vial of an experimental Ebola vaccine.

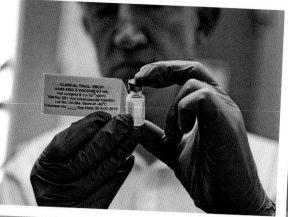

Thousands of people lost family members during the 2014 Ebola outbreak.

What the Future Holds

The 2014 Ebola outbreak in West Africa was the worst the world has ever seen. Past outbreaks have been isolated. They claimed a few hundred lives and then disappeared. The current outbreak has killed thousands of people in Africa, and it is not over yet. For the first time, the disease has also traveled to countries outside Africa. What does this mean for the future? How can we make sure a serious Ebola outbreak doesn't happen again?

Paths for Outbreak

One reason this outbreak was so bad is that it started in an area that was not remote and isolated. Roads allowed people to travel to other villages and cross borders between countries. The lack of protective clothing and supplies led to infections among health-care workers. It also took time for doctors to realize that the sickness they were seeing was Ebola. Before governments realized what was happening, the Ebola virus was already spreading far and wide.

Once Ebola was identified, health-care workers received special training and used protective clothing to keep from catching the disease.

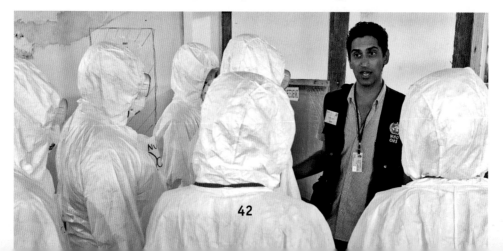

42

Workers continue to educate the people of rural Africa about the dangers of the Ebola virus.

Staying Safe

Training health-care workers to recognize Ebola symptoms and giving them the supplies they need to protect themselves will help contain future outbreaks. Other developments should also aid in controlling Ebola. Identifying which animal is the reservoir host could help experts predict where future outbreaks might start. And perhaps newly developed drugs will be able to cure or prevent the illness. The 2014 outbreak was devastating, but it is hopefully the last one the world will ever see. ★

True Statistics

Number of health-care workers who contracted Ebola in West Africa in 2014: 825

Number of those health-care workers who died in 2014: 493

Number of bats killed and eaten each year in the African country of Ghana: More than 100,000

Number of drugs currently being developed to treat Ebola: More than 12

Number of airports in the U.S. that screened arriving travelers for Ebola in 2014: 5

Did you find the truth?

(F) The Ebola virus can be spread only among humans.

(T) The 2014 Ebola outbreak in West Africa was the worst one in history.

Resources

Books

Draper, Allison. *Ebola*. New York: Rosen, 2002.

Hirschmann, Kris. *The Ebola Virus*. Detroit: Lucent Books/Thomson Gale, 2007.

Visit this Scholastic Web site for more information on Ebola:
★ www.factsfornow.scholastic.com
Enter the keyword **Ebola**

Important Words

cremating (KREE-may-ting) burning a dead body to ashes

diagnose (dye-uhg-NOHS) determine what disease a patient has or what the cause of a problem is

epidemic (ep-uh-DEM-ik) an infectious disease present in a large number of people at the same time

host (HOHST) an animal or plant on which a different animal lives

isolated (EYE-suh-lay-tid) alone or separate

primates (PRYE-mayts) members of the group of mammals that includes monkeys, apes, and humans

quarantined (KWOR-uhn-teend) keeping a person, animal, or plant away from others for a period of time to stop a disease from spreading

vaccines (vak-SEENZ) substances injected or taken orally that protect people from a particular disease

virus (VYE-ruhs) a tiny organism that can reproduce and grow only when inside living cells; viruses cause diseases such as polio, measles, the common cold, and AIDS

Index

Page numbers in **bold** indicate illustrations.

About the Author

Ann O. Squire is a psychologist and an animal behaviorist. Before becoming a writer, she studied the behavior of rats, tropical fish in the Caribbean, and electric fish from central Africa. Her favorite part of being a writer is the chance to learn as much as she can about all sorts of topics. In addition to *Ebola* and books on other health topics, Dr. Squire has written about many different animals, from lemmings to leopards and cicadas to cheetahs. She lives in Long Island City, New York.